AF126341

BOOK ANALYSIS

By Tara Dorrell

Interview with the Vampire

BY ANNE RICE

ANNE RICE

AMERICAN WRITER

- **Born in New Orleans in 1941.**
- **Notable works:**
  - *The Vampire Lestat* (1985), novel
  - *The Witching Hour* (1990), novel
  - *The Wolf Gift* (2012), novel

Born in New Orleans in 1941, Anne Rice is best known for her series *The Vampire Chronicles*. She became a PhD candidate in Literature at the University of California, Berkeley in 1966, but interrupted her studies after becoming disenchanted with the course, eventually finishing them with a course in Creative Writing at San Francisco State University in 1972.

Her daughter Michele passed away from leukaemia in 1972, and it was in the grief that followed that Rice started to rework a short story into what would eventually become *Interview with the Vampire*. Michele was reportedly the inspiration for the character of Claudia. Many of Rice's works focus on the supernatural, with others in the historical or religious genres. She is also known for her erotic fiction and her memoir *Called Out of Darkness: A Spiritual Confession* (2008).

INTERVIEW WITH THE VAMPIRE

THE ICONIC SOUTHERN GOTHIC VAMPIRE NOVEL

- **Genre:** gothic horror novel
- **Reference edition:** Rice, A. (2008) *Interview with the Vampire*. London: Sphere.
- **1st edition:** 1976
- **Themes:** the supernatural, horror, Christianity, good and evil, manipulation, lust, immortality

Anne Rice's *Interview with the Vampire* is a work of Southern Gothic horror that follows the life of plantation owner Louis de Pointe du Lac following his transformation into a vampire. Anne Rice used this novel to create a more empathetic vampire, with human emotions and motivations, unlike the callous, unfeeling vampires typically depicted in popular fiction. Rice draws on many of the tropes that are now considered typical of the vampire genre, such as sleeping in a coffin and a tormented, brooding protagonist. However,

Interview with the Vampire is actually one of the works that cemented these ideas in the modern literary imagination. While they may be overused today, it is in this context that many of them first appeared. *Interview with the Vampire* is the first in a series of books titled *The Vampire Chronicles*, and is followed by *The Vampire Lestat*.

The work received mixed reviews upon its publication, with some critics finding it sensually rich while others saw it as little more than poorly-disguised erotica. In 1994 it was adapted into a film of the same name starring Tom Cruise, Brad Pitt and Antonio Banderas. Three comics have also been made of the novel, in 1992, 1994 and 2012.

SUMMARY

THE ORIGINS OF LOUIS

Written in the first person, *Interview with a Vampire* is narrated by Louis de Pointe du Lac, a 200-year-old vampire who is recalling his life to a reporter, known only as "the boy" (p. 1). Louis begins his tale in 1791, with the death of his brother, Paul. Paul was an extraordinarily religious man, and Louis and Paul had quarrelled over the latter's desire to go to France to "turn the tide against atheism and the revolution" (p. 4). Paul had walked out, only to be found moments later with his neck snapped, having fallen down the stairs. Wracked with guilt and grief, Louis seeks death, yet cannot find it in him to kill himself. It is then that he is attacked by the vampire Lestat de Lioncourt, who drinks his blood before transforming Louis into a vampire himself. Now undead and immortal, Louis becomes Lestat's eternal companion, living on his own plantation with Lestat in the hopes that he will be taught what it means to be a vampire. Instead, he finds

Lestat to be cruel, selfish, and cunning, and far more comfortable with killing than Louis is. While Louis feeds on animal blood, Lestat takes pleasure in killing humans, befriending his victims and drawing out the process for his own amusement. Louis despises his companion, feeling himself to be superior, but is prevented from leaving when Lestat convinces him he holds knowledge about their state of which Louis knows nothing. Eventually the plantation slaves revolt against their supernatural masters, fearing their power. Louis and Lestat set fire to the plantation and kill any remaining slaves to preserve their secret, before fleeing to the local Freniere plantation, and then on to New Orleans.

Louis is careful to maintain control of their finances, disgusted by Lestat's opulent tastes, while also attempting to keep himself free from Lestat to some extent. Although Louis despises the practice, he slowly starts to concede to Lestat's influence, and feeds on humans while continuing to abhor his companion's lack of empathy for mortals. One night he comes across a five-year-old girl and her dead mother, and is unable to stop himself feeding off her.

Louis had been on the verge of leaving Lestat, having realised that he does not actually hold any knowledge about their kind. To prevent him from leaving, Lestat turns the child into a vampire, creating a daughter for them both as well as a reason for Louis to stay. Claudia, as they call her, swiftly takes to killing; she seduces and plays with her victims like Lestat does, much to his delight. However, she nonetheless remains closer to Louis, who attempts to educate her with mortal pursuits: art, literature and music. Although she is highly intelligent and as mature as an adult woman mentally, she is cursed to forever remain trapped in the body of a child. After 60 years of this, she grows angry at her body's inability to mature, and blames Lestat for her condition. She poisons him and slits his throat before Louis dumps his body in a swamp, but as she and Louis prepare to leave for Europe, Lestat reappears, having survived the murder attempt. Louis is forced to fight him, and eventually burns down the house with Lestat inside. He and Claudia then flee to Europe, seeking other vampires and knowledge about their origin, nature, and purpose in the world.

FLIGHT TO EUROPE

The pair arrive in eastern Europe, believing it to be the place of origin for all vampires. They travel across the continent, but instead of finding vampires like themselves, educated and refined, they only find decaying, animated corpse-like creatures. Discouraged and disillusioned, Louis and Claudia travel to Paris, where they take an extravagant hotel room. Although they are initially unable to locate other vampires, one night Louis encounters a couple of vampires who are as sophisticated as him and Claudia. They are invited to the Théâtre des Vampires, where they watch a coven of vampires feed on their mortal victims in front of an audience, who believe that it is all an elaborate act. They are later taken backstage to meet the coven: Santiago, Celeste, Estelle, and Armand, who at 400 years is the oldest vampire in existence. Claudia takes a dislike to the theatre vampires, feeling threatened by their presence and disgusted by their performance. Louis, however, feels drawn to Armand, fascinated with the vampire whom he believes will be able to answer the questions Lestat could not. Convinced Louis will leave her for Armand, Claudia persuades him to turn a dollmaker named Madeleine into a vampire, to be her companion if and when he leaves. He does so, and for a while the three uneasily coexist in the hotel.

LESTAT'S REVENGE

One night, the theatre vampires abduct them and take them to the theatre – where Lestat is waiting, having survived the fire in New Orleans. Santiago and Celeste had already been convinced that Louis and Claudia had killed another vampire, their master no less, which is viewed as is a capital crime. Lestat only confirms their suspicions, seeking revenge on Claudia. Thus, Louis is locked away in a coffin, while Claudia and Madeleine are tied up outside to be burned alive by the sun. Armand frees Louis, but is too late to save Claudia, and Louis finds only the ashen remains of her and Madeleine.

Now seeking revenge, Louis warns Armand to leave, and the next night sets fire to the theatre, using a scythe to kill any vampire that tries to escape. He and Armand then travel across Europe and the Mediterranean together, but the connection between them quickly wanes. Armand eventually convinces Louis to return to New Orleans in the 1920s by revealing that Lestat did not actually die in the theatre fire. Louis visits his old companion and finds him a shell of his former self, feeding only on animals as Louis had once done. Afterwards, Armand reveals that he was responsible for killing Claudia, believing that once she was gone Louis would become his companion, a connection to mortal life given his mortal sentiments and emotions. However, following Claudia's death, all his passion and emotion dissolved, and he remains indifferent both in his visit to Lestat and to Armand's revelations. Disappointed in his companion, now no different to every other vampire, Armand leaves.

Despite having concluded his tale, the reporter interviewing him remains unsatisfied, and instead demands Louis turns *him* into a vampire, to be his new companion. Disgusted that the boy has apparently learned nothing, Louis attacks him before leaving him for dead. The novel ends with the boy still alive and preparing to find Lestat.

CHARACTER STUDY

LOUIS DE POINTE DU LAC

Born in France but raised in New Orleans, Louis de Pointe du Lac is a handsome man who attracts the attention of Lestat with first his physical beauty ("brilliant green eyes" (p. 1) and dark hair), then with his tenderness and tragic life. The entire narrative is told from Louis' perspective as he recalls just some of the events of his immortal life. Considering how literally heartless the other vampires are, it is interesting that he is not as evil as them, but is in fact concerned with the matters of good and evil. However, it does mean he is lacking as a vampire, unable to reach his full potential as Claudia swiftly does.

As a mere 25-year-old man when he is turned, Louis is conflicted about who he is and his place in the world – and after his brother's death, he also begins to question his relationship with God. Once made immortal, his questions only increase in number as he becomes concerned with the ethics of being a vampire. These are questions that Lestat remains unconcerned with, but for Louis they are a driving force, even if other vampires consider him "flawed" (p. 194) for his obsession with them. Despite this, the vampire recalling his tale to us as our narrator does so with a level of apathy, with only slight flashes of diluted emotion showing at intervals. It is a drastic change from the emotional Louis we know for majority of the novel, which thus becomes a tale of how he lost his human sentiment and became as cold and indifferent as every other vampire.

Louis' relationship with his maker is fraught from the beginning, as he despises Lestat's disregard for mortal life and inability to see any beauty in mortal creations. Nevertheless, the two live together almost as a couple, with undertones of sensuality to their relationship that are present in all of Louis' other relationships – "it is like love" (p. 24). Until the end of the novel, he acts as a foil to the all the other cold, heartless vampires. While he might adore her, he is essentially the antithesis of Claudia, who fully embraces her vampiric nature from the start, never really knowing what it is to be human. His relationship with Claudia walks the line between being familial and sensual. He sees them as both "father and daughter" (p. 78) and "lover and lover" (*ibid*.), and the confusion can be somewhat justified – she is, after all, an adult woman in a child's body. Upon meeting the Parisian vampires, Louis becomes enamoured with Armand, thinking he has found in him someone who could give him the information Lestat was unable to. He eventually chooses Armand over Claudia, although it is clear that his love with his "human nature" (p. 91) for her was maintaining his humanity. His relationship with Armand disintegrates rapidly after this is gone.

CLAUDIA

Introduced as a five-year-old girl, Claudia is cursed to remain that way as long as she lives. She becomes the adoptive daughter of Lestat and Louis, utterly vampiric in nature in a manner Louis never fully achieves, and like Lestat takes pleasure in her kills. She uses her child-like appearance to seduce mortals into helping her, befriending and loving them before feeding on them. For this, Lestat adores her, while Louis attempts to introduce her to more mortal pleasures in "reading the work of Aristotle" (p. 77) or "pecking out the music of Mozart" (*ibid*.).

However, her relationship with her pseudo-fathers becomes wracked with tension as she grows older in her mind, but remains childlike in form. She is often described as having "a woman's eyes" (p. 72), and Rice uses purposefully sensual language when depicting her movements. Louis fears her to be "less human" (p. 115) than any of them, the result of being only five years old when she was turned. As she and Louis travel across the continent, it becomes clear that she holds the same intelligence and manipulative skills as Lestat, all with the appearance of a delicate little child. While Louis is enamoured with her, it is unclear whether she ever feels quite the same or only loves him because of his uses to her and the familiarity he provides. While he truly loves her, she both loves and hates him in equal measure, unable to ignore her nature as a vampire. A wedge grows between them in Europe, and this tension is only heightened by her demand that Louis turn a woman into a vampire to be her replacement companion when he leaves her. When Claudia and her companion are burnt alive following Lestat's reappearance in Paris, her death proves to be Louis' undoing, driving him to truly become a cold creature of the night.

LESTAT DE LIONCOURT

Depicted as a beautiful man with blond hair and deathly pale skin, Lestat is the vampire who transforms Louis, and is also his companion for the first half of the novel. Louis comes to believe pretty early on that is superior to Lestat, who has no concern with mortality. Lestat enjoys killing for the sake of it; he relishes toying with his victims and finds feeding on humans exhilarating. He is also obsessed with pretty things, which is one of his reasons for turning Louis and loving Claudia. It aggravates him that Louis refuses to place any property in his name, effectively keeping Lestat under his control to some extent. Lestat is manipulative, cruel and selfish, hence Louis' and later Claudia's hatred of him. No matter how often they try to escape him, he truly does live up to the term 'immortal' – not only is he a vampire (and therefore undead) throughout, but he manages to survive being poisoned and having his throat sliced open, and escapes two burning buildings.

The last time Louis sees Lestat, he is a mere shadow of his former self, refusing to eat anything but animals and essentially dying of old age very,

very slowly. The end of the novel shows a contrast in how he and Louis have developed: while the latter has become colder and abandoned his mortal sentiments, it seems Lestat has recovered them, desperate for Louis' companionship and no longer feeding on humans, as Louis had once done. *Interview with the Vampire* is followed by a sequel centred on Lestat, entitled *The Vampire Lestat*.

ARMAND

Armand is a quiet but alluring vampire whom Louis and Claudia meet in Paris. He is the head of a coven of vampires who live at the Théâtre des Vampires, and as far as he is aware, is the oldest vampire in existence at 400 years old. He quickly becomes enamoured with Louis, but is thoughtful and considerate towards him – a stark contrast to Lestat. However, in reality he is no less manipulative, and drives a wedge between Louis and Claudia. He is convinced that in Louis he can find a way of becoming more a part of the mortal world, given how mortal Louis acts. He eventually burns Claudia and her consort alive, saving Louis and leaving France with him.

The two travel together briefly before Armand convinces him to return to New Orleans. It is here that he leaves Louis, who no longer cares, because since Claudia's death he has become completely apathetic. Armand had hoped that by telling Louis he had killed her, or by showing him how pathetic Lestat had become, he would get some emotional rise out of the man, but Louis' passion and human emotion died with Claudia. Although he only appears towards the end of the novel, Armand is a prominent character in the following books in Rice's *The Vampire Chronicles* series.

ANALYSIS

RELIGIOUS UNDERTONES

Over the course of the novel there are many references to and associations with Christianity, and Louis becomes obsessed with the questions of good and evil, and whether or not vampires are the children of Satan. This begins with his brother's death. Paul was an extremely religious man, and after he dies Louis begins to question whether he was too swift in brushing off his brother's visions – should he have believed the religious fervour? So begins his questioning of Christianity, which never really stops. The very idea of having a creator who is not God creates all kinds of questions for Louis and the reader, while Rice's equation of being turned into a vampire with rebirth is almost biblical. It is when he meets Armand that all of Louis' religious concerns come to light, as he believes the older vampire will have answers for him. Armand is able to reassure him that they are not the children of Satan, and claims that even if they are, God made Satan, which in turn makes them the children of God.

Several scenes have starkly religious undertones, and although the vampires may be cold-hearted killers, there is something almost godly in their power. One of the clearest instances of this is in the church scene, where Louis is highly conscious that *he* is the only supernatural being in the church. In that moment he is truly aware that there is no religious being to save the priest from death. Although Louis attempts to repent, he ends up killing the man instead, his supernatural power conquering any religious authority that might have existed. As human as Louis often appears, especially in comparison to the other vampires, when he seeks the revenge for Claudia's murder, he appears to embody death itself: an undead being bringing destruction to creatures considered immortal, armed with fire and fury and, of course, a scythe.

Rice's own religious leanings are examined in the novel: in using the Deep South of America as her location, she is able to draw on the religious fervour that she herself would have been familiar with, given her Catholic upbringing in New Orleans. Over the course of her life Anne Rice has had a highly religious childhood followed by years of atheism, a return to Christianity, and then a departure from Christianity but not from Christ. Although *Interview with the Vampire* was published during her years as an atheist, the conflict Louis feels potentially mirrors her own.

EROTIC TENSIONS

Although there is nothing explicitly sexual in the novel, it is filled with erotic undertones between almost all the characters. The relationships always have a clear dominant figure – Lestat's control of Louis gives the impression that he almost owns him, which in turn means that the slave uprising foreshadows Louis and Claudia's own rebellion against their creator. The very physical act of drinking someone else's blood instigates the aggression in the relationships here, and goes on to almost become a substitute for sexual intercourse.

The relationship between vampires and humans is also notably sexual, with several of the mortal characters becoming sexually aroused at the thought of being bitten by a vampire. The most prominent example of this is when Louis bites Denis, the young boy belonging to Armand. As he bites him, Louis is fully aware of "the hard strength of his sex beneath his clothes" (p. 176). The imagery that follows, of the boy's "gasping" (*ibid*.) and "his ecstasy, his conscious pleasure" (*ibid*.) only heightens this sexual nature of the scene. While Louis finds Lestat to be the dominant figure in their relationship, all humans can be dominated by vampires, theirs for the taking. The 'show' the theatre vampires put on is morbidly sexual, a graphic scene of a woman being stripped and her blood being sucked by multiple vampires, all in front of an assuming audience. Her naked figure is repeatedly emphasised, and the revulsion of Louis and Claudia echoes our own.

The relationship between Louis and Claudia is also fraught with erotic tensions. It is difficult to know whether they play the roles of father and daughter or of two lovers, all of these terms being used at various points throughout the novel. They share a coffin for the majority of the book, and when Louis becomes infatuated with Armand, Claudia's reaction is akin to that of a jealous lover. She is fully aware of how she can manipulate humans before she feeds on them, and seems to manipulate louis in the same way – once turned she is never the innocent little girl he so often mistakes her for, although even he notes there is something "dreadfully sensual about her" (p. 79).

Louis' relationship with Armand is easily comparable to that of lovers, and indeed he does say several times that he "could love Armand" (p. 247), while Armand himself states that he wants Louis "more than anything" (p. 220). Initially it appears they have a deeper level of connection that Louis and Lestat, given that theirs comes from a lust for the knowledge the other contains. However, their relationship swiftly fizzles out following Claudia's death and Louis' subsequent loss of passion.

GOTHIC HORROR

Th gothic horror genre originated in the 18th century, and often includes the trope of the antihero, along with the themes of death, the supernatural, and occasionally romance. One of the key elements to any gothic horror novel is the feeling of dread throughout – the feeling of foreboding, that something worse is coming.

Anne Rice includes several instances of foreshadowing that exacerbate this – for example, the slave uprising on the plantation at the start of the novel is later mimicked in Louis and Claudia's uprising against Lestat, who is essentially their own slave master. The play the theatre vampires put on later comes back to haunt them in the form of a vengeful Louis, who burns them alive while armed with a scythe, a figure of death itself.

Rice does reject some typical tropes associated with vampires at the start of the novel – Louis asks Lestat whether they are affected by garlic, or the crucifix. While Rice's vampires are impervious to such items, their traditional use in gothic fiction is emphasised in eastern Europe, where terrified villagers attempt to ward off the corpse-like zombies with such items. The scenes could have come straight out of any 18th-century work of gothic horror, and contrast with the elegant lifestyle Louis, Lestat and Claudia lived in New Orleans.

Much of the ideas about vampires that Rice uses have become common to the point of being clichéd today, yet it was in *Interview with the*

Vampire that many of them were consolidated as being a part of vampiric lore. The use of coffins is particularly notable, as is the consistently black attire – the theatre vampires even dye their hair black to continue to match their aesthetic.

FURTHER REFLECTION

SOME QUESTIONS TO THINK ABOUT...

- How does the narrative perspective change our reading of the novel?
- Compare Louis' relationship with Lestat to his relationship with Armand.
- How does the 1994 film adaptation compare to the novel?
- Explore the relevance of Louis and Claudia's time in eastern Europe.
- Why do you think Rice chose to base the majority of novel in New Orleans and Paris?
- How does Louis' attachment to his humanity drive the novel?
- Examine how Louis changes over the course of the novel – do you think it is for the better?
- How does Anne Rice subvert or emphasise typical tropes of gothic horror vampire fiction?
- Explore the importance of religion in the novel.

We want to hear from you!
Leave a comment on your online library
and share your favourite books on social media!

FURTHER READING

REFERENCE EDITION

- Rice, A. (2008) *Interview with the Vampire.* London: Sphere.

REFERENCE STUDIES

- Jackson, L. (2014) An Effigy of Intimacy: Sexuality in *Interview with the Vampire. Blue Stockings Society.* [Online]. [Accessed 23 February 2019]. Available from: <http://www.blue-stockings.org/?p=186>
- Tadlock, J. (No date) *Religion in the Vampire Motif.* [Online]. [Accessed 23 February 2019]. Available from: <http://justintadlock.com/writing/religion-in-the-vampire-motif>

ADDITIONAL SOURCES

- Haggerty, G. (1998) Anne Rice and the Queering of Culture. *Novel: A Forum on Fiction.* [Online]. [Accessed 23 February 2019]. Available from: <https://www.jstor.org/stable/1346054?se-q=2#metadata_info_tab_contents>

ADAPTATIONS

- *Interview with the Vampire.* (1994) [Film]. Neil Jordan. Dir. United States: Warner Bros. Pictures.

Bright ≡Summaries.com

www.brightsummaries.com

Ebook EAN: 9782808018890

Paperback EAN: 9782808018906

Legal Deposit: D/2019/12603/111

Cover: © Primento

Digital conception by Primento, the digital partner of publishers.